MORE THAN EARTHLINGS

An astronaut's thoughts for Christ-centered living

JAMES B. IRWIN

BROADMAN PRESS
Nashville, Tennessee

Except as otherwise noted, all Scripture quotations are from the HOLY BIBLE *New International Version,* copyright © 1978, New York Bible Society. Used by permission.

All Scripture quotations marked KJV are from the King James Version of the Bible.

All Scripture quotations marked RSV are from the Revised Standard Version of the Bible, copyrighted 1946, 1952 © 1971, 1973.

Dewey Decimal Classification: 242
Subject Heading: MEDITATIONS
Library of Congress Catalog Card Number: 83-070369
Printed in the United States of America

If you wish to contact Colonel James B. Irwin, his address is High Flight Foundation, P.O. Box 1387, Colorado Springs, Colorado 80901—Phone: (303)576-7700.

DEDICATION

This book is dedicated to all the inhabitants of planet Earth who will never fly into outer space and also to those who will. May these pages bring renewed inspiration to your soul as you reach for the stars. When my flight to the moon was completed, I realized that I had an obligation to all the people of the blue planet Earth. I had been given much and realized much more was required of me. I am your servant. May I share the love of God with you?

ACKNOWLEDGMENT

I wish to acknowledge the tireless and fruitful efforts of my writer, Monte Unger. We have been friends since the beginning of High Flight Foundation, but this is our first opportunity to work together on a book. I am glad that I found Monte to help with *More Than Earthlings*. I am also glad that Monte found me after my disastrous mishap on the north face of Mount Ararat while we were searching for Noah's ark!

Introduction

I am now more than an earthling, because I have walked on the moon. Being on the moon had a profound spiritual impact upon my life. Before I entered space with the Apollo 15 mission in July of 1971, I was a lukewarm Christian, to say the least! I was even a silent Christian, but I feel the Lord sent me to the moon so I could return to the earth and share his Son, Jesus Christ.

The entire space achievement is put in proper perspective when one realizes that *God walking on the earth* is more important than man walking on the moon. I believe that God walked on the earth 2,000 years ago in the person of Jesus Christ. I have totally yielded my life to the Lord's service to tell people everywhere about the life-changing message of Christ.

God wishes to continue his walk on the earth today, and he does it through your life and mine. He calls each of us to be his servant. God loves you and wants you to enter into this most precious relationship and fellowship with him.

You can be "more than an earthling," not by going into space, but by submitting yourself to the Lord. Admit your sins, acknowledge your need of him, open your life to God's perfect forgiveness, and accept Jesus Christ into your life as your Lord and Savior. This is the first step to a new life—a life with supernatural power and filled with abundance. Jesus declares, "I am come that they might have life, and that they might have it more abundantly" (John 10:10, KJV).

Dostoevski observed that everyone spends his entire life searching for someone or something to believe in. Some find the answer. Many do not. I believe that Jesus Christ is the answer for each and every person.

During our moon walk we found the only pure, white rock which has been brought back from the moon. It was immediately labeled the "Genesis" rock by the press corps in

Houston. The Bible tells of a white rock in Revelation 2:17, "To him who overcomes, I will give some of the hidden manna. I will also give him a white stone with a new name written on it, known only to him who receives it."

How I pray for earthlings that they might know the joy of a new life with Christ, that each might have a new name indicating the beginning of a new life, and that each will be more than an earthling. You, too, can share in the greatest news ever to reach the blue planet earth.

My first book, still in print, is entitled *To Rule the Night*. This title came from Genesis 1:16, "And God made two great lights; the greater light to rule the day, and the lesser light to rule the night; he made the stars also" (KJV). God made the moon to cast light into the physical darkness of mankind's night. Then many years later he sent his Son Jesus to the earth, bringing light into the spiritual darkness of man.

I have traveled a long road in my search for light and truth—and still have a long way to go; but in the pages of this book I wish to share that greatest of all discoveries with you: a new life in Christ! You *can* be more than an earthling!

This book will share spiritual principles of the Christian life using analogies from space. When I retired from the space program to begin ministering for the Lord, I had reservations about starting yet another Christian organization, because there were so many already effectively serving Christ. I prayed about it and asked for advice from such men as Dr. Billy Graham. He encouraged me by saying, "The possibilities are so unique that you need your own organization." With that, we formed High Flight. We had a "high flight" when we travelled over half a million miles to the moon and back, but we all can have even a higher flight here on earth as men and women committed to living for Christ. This will give complete assurance for our highest flight when we leave earth.

JAMES B. IRWIN

Contents

1
How to Handle Fame

It was a tremendous shock returning from the moon and becoming an instant celebrity, a hero, a sort of superman. When I asked my wife what she wanted my first book, *To Rule the Night,* to do, she answered firmly, "I want it to break down a myth in people's eyes that Astronauts are infallible. They are not gods. They are human beings. They are part of families; they have wives and children. They have the same emotions, the same needs, and the same feelings as everyone else has."

A Christian can gain "fame" in any number of degrees: from garnering a business award to a teenager winning his event in a track meet. The result in the person's spirit is the same: pride. How will he handle this pride? It is what he does with the adulation and attention that is important. "For who makes you different from anyone else? What do you have that you did not receive? And if you did receive it, why do you boast as though you did not?" (1 Cor. 4:7).

The act you do isn't what exalts you in God's eyes. He is looking for humility. Jesus taught, "Whoever exalts himself will be humbled, and whoever humbles himself will be exalted" (Matt. 23:12, RSV). Man cannot lift himself up and then try to make something of himself by saying, "Look at me . . . see what I've done." It is just the opposite for the Christian: "Humble yourselves before the Lord, and he will lift you up" (Jas. 4:10).

I must admit that the instant fame was extremely difficult to handle. But during the ticker-tape parade in New York City, with Mayor John Lindsay sitting on my feet so I wouldn't fall out of the limousine, I realized that I had to become a servant to all these people, to all those across America, and those around the world. Because I had been privileged to travel into space and see the earth from a new perspective, I had to become a servant of all. I said, "Lord, here is my life. Use me as your servant to help reach a hungry world." Now my life has more purpose than ever, and I have begun my most strategic mission: to tell earthlings about salvation in Christ.

MORE THAN EARTHLINGS

New York City gave the Apollo 15 astronauts a tumultuous welcome (National Aeronautics and Space Administration Photo).

2
Instant Availability to God's Call

The call was out for more Astronauts. I thought, *Why not?* The call came in February, and I was nearly thirty-six—in March I would be at the age limit. I took the tests and the interviews. Soon afterwards Deke Slayton, the NASA Director of Astronauts, telephoned me at my Colorado Springs office. "Jim, would you like to come down to Houston?" This was an invitation to be part of the Astronaut program. "I'm ready, Deke," I answered. "When do you want me?" I was ready immediately.

The story is told of General George S. Patton who was stationed in 1942 at the Desert Training Center in California. One morning at 10:45 he received a telephone call telling him that General George Marshall wanted him to report to Washington D.C. as soon as he could leave the Center. The only other information he had was that he was to prepare for a long absence and that he might never return to the Desert Training Center. Patton arrived in Washington the *same day* and was escorted directly to General Marshall.

Many men are ready to respond to a mission: in business, politics, the military, and especially in the Astronaut program. Once we were Astronauts, our response was that we were always ready and able to do anything. We always said, "We are ready, no matter what you want us to do." But are we ready when God calls?

Isaiah was. "Then I heard the voice of the Lord saying,

'Whom shall I send? And who will go for us?' And I said, 'Here am I. Send me!' " (Isa. 6:8).

The disciples were ready to follow Jesus. Matthew 4:18-22 states:

> *As Jesus was walking beside the Sea of Galilee, he saw two brothers, Simon called Peter and his brother Andrew. They were casting a net into the lake, for they were fishermen. "Come, follow me," Jesus said, "and I will make you fishers of men." At once they left their nets and followed him. Going on from there, he saw two other brothers, James the son of Zebedee and his brother John. They were in a boat with their father Zebedee, preparing their nets. Jesus called them, and immediately they left the boat and their father and followed him.*

Will you be ready when God calls you?

3
The Eyes of Man Are Never Full

When we blasted off, I was absolutely dedicated to the challenge of achieving a perfect flight. I was thinking only about the scientific aspect; I had no notion whatsoever of the spiritual voyage. It would have been beyond my wildest imagination to guess that this flight would not satisfy me, that I would come back to earth a different person, bound for a higher flight.

My search before the flight was to go high and fast—and, hopefully, to go into space. And if I were really fortunate, maybe to reach the moon. I thought that would be the ultimate. But I realized after it was all over that it didn't satisfy. "Death and destruction are never satisfied, and neither are the eyes of man" (Prov. 27:20).

Some have gone to the moon and come back in deep depression, a nervous breakdown in one case. He couldn't sense a purpose in life after reaching the moon. The moon signified the ultimate. There wasn't anything to match that.

Matthew 16:26 says, "For what is a man profited, if he shall gain the whole world, and lose his own soul?" (KJV).

What *does* satisfy is knowing the love of the Lord and having him close for direction and guidance. I began to realize that the flight to the moon was only the beginning. It was simply one step which opened many doors for greater service, service to God and to people all over the earth.

Now I can testify with the Psalmist, "But it is good for me to draw near to God: I have put my trust in the Lord God, that I may declare all thy works" (Ps. 73:28, KJV).

The Apollo 15 mission began with the lift-off of an Apollo/ Saturn V space vehicle (NASA Photo).

4
God Has a Plan for You

When we blasted off for the moon, one would think that all the odds were against us. We planned to land in a precise spot on a moving target 238,000 miles away. The moon is not only revolving around the earth at 2,300 miles per hour, but the earth is revolving around the sun at 66,000 miles per hour. The earth is spinning on its axis once each twenty-four hours, and we had to attain the speed of 25,000 miles per hour to escape the pull of earth's gravity. How could we compute all this motion so we would land at an exact place on the moon?

We could do it because God manages the universe with infinite precision, controlling all the motions of the planets and the stars. We could depend upon his laws. We used God's precision to perfect our rendezvous. And as God has a perfect plan for outer space, so does he have a perfect plan for the inner space of man—the spirit of man.

While I was on the moon, God was with me—as much as he is on earth—working out his plan for my life. Psalm 139:8-10 says, "If I go up to the heavens, you are there; if I make my bed in the depths, you are there. If I rise on the wings of the dawn, if I settle on the far side of the sea, even there your hand will guide me, your right hand will hold me fast."

As with the seemingly impossible odds to hit a pinpointed landing spot on the moon, it seems just as impossible to make life on earth function smoothly. Alvin Toffler wrote in *The Third Wave,* describing the current state of man, "A powerful tide is surging across much of the world today, creating a new, often bizarre, environment in which to work, play, marry, raise children or retire. In this bewildering context, businessmen swim against highly erratic economic currents; politicians see their ratings bob wildly up and down; universities, hospitals, and other institutions battle desperately against inflation. Value systems splinter and crash while the lifeboats of family, church, and state are hurled madly about"[1]

Yet God has designed peace as part of his plan for our lives. Jesus promises, "Peace I leave with you; my peace I give you. I do not give to you as the world gives. Do not let your hearts be troubled and do not be afraid" (John 14:27). We can trust his plan for our lives!

NOTE

1. Alvin Toffler, *The Third Wave* (New York: William Morrow and Co., Inc., 1980), pp. 17-18.

5
Are You in Contact with God?

Often during our space flight, these words were spoken:

Houston Control: "How do you read Houston?"
Astronauts: "Houston, we read you loud and clear."

If we hadn't replied in that manner, Houston would've known something was wrong. Communications would have been broken. A problem would have been hindering our contact.

Sin has broken man's communications with God. Isaiah 59:2 says, "But your iniquities have separated you from your God; your sins have hidden his face from you, so that he will not hear."

Does this mean man is eternally doomed? Is there a way to take these sins away? Do we have a chance?

When we were ready to leave the moon, our CAPCOM at Mission Control, Joe Allen, quoted part of a poem, "We are ready for you to come back again to the homes of men on the cool green hills of earth."

God wants us with him. He will not desert us . . . he has provided a way of rescue.

6
God Never Deserts You

If the Lunar Module's ascent engine would have failed, Dave Scott and I would still be on the moon. Dead. There would have been no time for a spaceship from earth to reach us before our oxygen supply would have been depleted; and the Command Module is not designed to land.

But God will never desert us. Man always has a chance. To explain this, I use a space-illustrated version of Campus Crusade's "Four Spiritual Laws."

First, *God loves you and has a wonderful plan for your life*. The highest flight man can have on earth is to understand this love and this personal plan. John 3:16 says, "For God so loved the world that he gave his one and only Son, that whoever believes in him shall not perish but have eternal life."

Second, *Man is sinful and separated from God, thus he cannot know and experience God's love and plan for his life*. Man's flight plan is marred because he is sinful and separated from God. This is much like being separated from the spaceship in a space walk. Man will die unless he is reconnected. Romans 3:23 says, "For all have sinned and fall short of the glory of God." And Romans 6:23 says, "For the wages of sin is death, but the gift of God is eternal life in Christ Jesus our Lord."

Third, *Jesus Christ is God's only provision for man's sin. Through him you can know and experience God's plan for your life*. This connecting link, like the umbilical cord on a space walk, between God and man is Jesus Christ. John 14:6

MORE THAN EARTHLINGS   **21**

Astronaut Worden went through his "spacewalk"—note the umbilical attachment *(NASA Photo)*.

says, "I am the way and the truth and the life. No one comes to the Father except through me." And 1 John 5:11-12 says, "God has given us eternal life, and this life is in his Son. He who has the Son has life; he who does not have the Son of God does not have life."

Fourth, *We must individually receive Jesus Christ as Savior and Lord—then we can know and experience God's love and plan for our lives.* The connecting link must be made personally. It isn't something someone else can do for us. It is intensely personal and private. Revelation 3:20 says, "Here I am! I stand at the door and knock. If anyone hears my voice and opens the door, I will go in and eat with him, and he with me." This is Christ speaking. Asking him into your life and believing that he will enter is what it means to personally accept him. Have you asked the Creator of the universe into your life?

7
Christ Can Hold Your Life Together

It wasn't easy to adjust to the weightlessness of space. Everything was restless. When our snaptop bags were open the slightest bit, things would start drifting out. Toothbrushes, tissues, cameras, and all sorts of items would float out and go in all directions.

This is how many of our lives are—drifting in all directions, because there is no central force holding us together.

America's number-one killer is heart disease, much of it caused by stress. We are tense and stressful because we as individuals are not integrated within ourselves. We are trying to hold all things together in our lives, but we can't. We need something else.

This is true because we are God-designed creatures, meant to relate to the Creator. But when Adam and Eve sinned in the Garden of Eden, things began flying apart, just like in the weightlessness of outer space. Man was banished from the garden; he had to work by the sweat of his brow; the woman gave birth in pain; Cain became the first murderer; and the state of mankind permanently changed.

Then mankind began its never-ending thirst to reconnect with God. It is as if I were on a space walk and became disconnected from the Command Module. I would drift away for eternity, but if I could somehow reconnect myself with the Command Module I would be saved.

God saw this dilemma in man and provided a way of rescue. It was by giving his own Son, Jesus Christ, to die for the sins of man (John 3:16, Rom. 5:8). The removal of this barrier of sin enables us once again to have daily, constant fellowship with God.

Christ personally comes to reside inside us, inside there where all that turmoil is. This changes us. Colossians 1:17 says, "He is before all things, and in Him all things hold together." The Lord not only holds the universe together, but he can hold us together individually.

A fragmented society made up of fragmented men and women can be held together by the adhesive of Jesus Christ.

The Apollo 15 crew gazed on the whole earth from outer space *(NASA Photo).*

8
How Important Is Money to You?

While traveling to the moon, we could look back and see earth, the beautiful blue planet. It looked like a Christmas tree ornament hanging motionless in space. It was mostly blue, shrouded with bands of white clouds, but we could see the warm, natural colors of the browns of the deserts and mountains and the greens of the vast jungles.

But we could not see any of the works of mankind—no cities, no lights, no monuments, no excavations—nothing. It was as if man didn't even exist. All of the riches, power, and strivings of man could not be seen from space.

Down here, because we are so close to the works of humans, we are awed. We feel the power. We crave the riches. It is so real—and so desirable. We are warned in Psalm 49:16-20:

> Do not be overawed when a man grows rich, when the splendor of his house increases; for he will take nothing with him when he dies, his splendor will not descend with him. Though while he lived he counted himself blessed— and men praise you when you prosper—he will join the generations of his fathers, who will never see the light of life. A man who has riches without understanding is like the beasts that perish.

The basic earthling continually yearns for more, and often that "more" belongs to someone else. This envy creates unnecessary tension and anxiety—stress that doesn't have to be. Paul said:

I have learned to be content whatever the circumstances. I know what it is to be in need, and I know what it is to have plenty. I have learned the secret of being content in any and every situation, whether well fed or hungry, whether living in plenty or in want (Phil. 4:11-12).

The secret of the contented life is found in Jesus Christ. He said, "I am come that they might have life, and that they might have it more abundantly" (John 10:10). He not only gives abundant life here on earth, but he gives eternal life. First John 5:11-12 says, "And this is the testimony: God has given us eternal life, and this life is in his Son. He who has the Son has life; he who does not have the Son of God does not have life."

9
Listen to Advice

We hadn't even landed on the moon, and already we had trouble. There was a water leak in one of the valves. Karl Henize, the Capsule Communicator at the time, listened to our description of the problem, then said, "Okay, stand by. Lots of people are thinking down here."

Then they gave us the help we needed:

Houston: "We suspect that the injector outlet is loose, and we have a procedure for tightening it up.

Apollo 15: "Okay, give it quick."

Houston: "Roger, we need tool number three and tool number W out of the tool kit."

Apollo 15: "Okay, three and W out of the tool kit."

Houston: "Right, put number three in the tool W ratchet, and insert tool three in the hex opening in the chlorine injector port."

Apollo 15: "Okay, that looks like where it's probably leaking."

Houston: "Once you've got tool number three well engaged in that injection port, turn it about a quarter of a turn."

The leak stopped!

Proverbs 19:20 says, "Listen to advice and accept instruction, and in the end you will be wise." We were not only wiser, but we stayed alive!

As we Astronauts in space could learn from those wiser

technicians and scientists on earth, so can we Christians can learn from those who are wiser in the knowledge of the Word of God. Proverbs 22:3 says, "A prudent man sees danger and takes refuge, but the simple keep going and suffer for it."

Even the wise man can still learn: "Instruct a wise man and he will be wiser still; teach a righteous man and he will add to his learning" (Prov. 9:9).

Learning from others is a continual process for the Christian.

10
No Man Is an Island

When we were in space, we always worked in conjunction with others. There were unseen tens of thousands in support positions on earth. Even in space we had a team of three. And two of us walked on the moon. Ecclesiastes 4:12 observes, "Though one may be overpowered, two can defend themselves. A cord of three strands is not quickly broken."

While Dave Scott and I were on the moon, Al Worden was circling the moon in the Command Module. He was always out there. We talked to him daily. He was our ride back to earth. Without him we would have been doomed, for our Lunar Module was not designed to fly through space and reenter the earth's atmosphere.

It is the same with Christians. We are each part of a greater body, and we function best by working with others. Man was not made to exist alone. Genesis 2:18 states, "The Lord God said, 'It is not good for the man to be alone. I will make a helper suitable for him.'" And poet John Donne left this classic phrase: "No man is an island." This is certainly obvious when mankind reaches out into space. It may not be as obvious in Christian fellowship, but it is just as true. Romans 12:5 says, "So in Christ we who are many form one body, and each member belongs to all the others."

This is one of the reasons why the central teaching force of Christianity is the bonding power of love. Love helps people get along peacefully with one another. Throughout history there have been wars and rumors of wars . . . there are wars

**Without Mission Control in Houston the Apollo 15 mission—
and other missions—could not have succeeded** *(NASA Photo).*

today, not only wars between nations, but petty wars between neighbors and businesses, between and within churches, and within families.

This is why it is necessary for Christ to reign in each person's heart. He is the great personification of love, and when he is present love is there. Matthew 18:20 says, "For where two or three come together in my name, there am I with them." Because we are relating beings, we need God's presence in our midst so we will relate as brothers, not as enemies.

11
We Need Others

We were flying at 3,400 mph just nine miles above the moon's surface. We didn't have any control over the spacecraft, and if we could have, we probably couldn't have reacted fast enough to miss the high mountains on the horizon. As we sped toward them we wondered if we would clear them. We assumed that Houston Control knew where the mountains were and how high they were.

We needed Houston!

Houston gave us a staggering amount of support. The backup people were constantly working with duplicates of all systems to solve problems we had not discovered yet.

Three verses in Proverbs tell us to rely on the counsel of many advisers: "Plans fail for lack of counsel, but with many advisers they succeed" (Prov. 15:22). "For lack of guidance a nation falls, but many advisers make victory sure" (Prov. 11:14). And, "For waging war you need guidance, and for victory many advisers" (Prov. 24:6).

Christians supernaturally have the Master Source, Jesus Christ, on whom they rely for guidance. But there are times when it is also necessary to ask the counsel of wiser and more mature Christian men and women in the fellowship. God works through his people.

This is part of the value of Christian fellowship. We are a body. We do work in conjunction with one another. Others may have experienced exactly the same thing you are going through, and will be able to offer valuable insight you hadn't considered.

12
The Providential Care of God

When the Lunar Module landed on the moon, it came to rest at a prominent angle because we landed on the rim of a small crater. Three legs were inside the crater, but the fourth leg was right on the rim. This was a little annoying, but it turned out to be providential protection. When we awakened the morning of our second day on the moon, Houston informed us the Lunar Module had lost twenty-five pounds of water the first day. This was far too much.

We checked and found a water leak. Naturally, the water had flowed to the lowest corner of the spacecraft, and fortunately this corner had no electrical connections. If the Lunar Module had been slanted the other way, the water would have flowed to the corner into a mass of electrical equipment. Most likely the water would have shorted the connections, which could have interfered with our communications and even our ability to lift off.

We would have been stranded. People have asked if another mission would have been sent up to rescue us. Even if there had been a spacecraft ready to go onto the pad, it still would have taken three days to get to the moon. We had oxygen for only one more day! If the leaking water would have caused us to be stranded, that would have been the end of us.

Another incident showed the providential care of God. Shortly after the next Apollo flight (Apollo 16) left the surface of the moon, a seismic device detected the impact of an object estimated to be ten feet in diameter. It hit very close to the scientific base and made a crater about the size of a football field. This showed that objects are still hitting the moon. If one had hit when and where Dave and I were exploring during the Apollo 15 mission . . . well . . .

"'There is no one like the God of Jeshurun, who rides on the heavens to help you and on the clouds in his majesty. The eternal God is your refuge, and underneath are the everlasting arms'" (Deut. 33:26-27).

13
Priorities

Something could have gone wrong at any time during our moon flight, so we had contingency plans at every stage.

The most important part of the mission was to collect rocks from the mountainous area of the moon. We made provisions to gather a contingency sample. Then if we had to leave abruptly, we would at least have some rocks. In fact, this was deemed more important than placing the American flag or erecting the scientific base.

As soon as we stepped out of the Lunar Module, we picked up our first moon sample and placed it in a spot so it would not be overlooked if we had to make a hasty departure. This had priority.

The entire Christian experience is based on priority systems, all the time, every day, in every small and large matter.

Do you put others first? In relationships what is most important, your needs or theirs? "Love . . . is not self-seeking" (1 Cor. 13:4). "Do nothing out of selfish ambition or vain conceit, but in humility consider others better than yourselves" (Phil. 2:3). "In everything, do to others what you would have them do to you" (Matt. 7:12). The Christian's priority system puts others first.

Do you give thanks in every situation? No matter what happens to you, "Give thanks in all circumstances, for this is God's will for you in Christ Jesus" (1 Thess. 5:18). The first reaction is not to grumble or complain, but to give thanks . . .

for this draws your attention to Christ and away from yourself.

Do you put God first in planning? Proverbs 3:5-6 says, "Trust in the Lord with all your heart and lean not on your own understanding; in all your ways acknowledge him, and he will make your paths straight."

Do you write that first check for the Lord? "Honor the Lord with your wealth, with the firstfruits of all your crops; then your barns will be filled to overflowing, and your vats will brim over with new wine" (Prov. 3:9-10).

Study the Bible and begin developing the priority system which God designed for you. It could change your life!

14
The Holy Spirit Is a Constant Companion

We had been out on the surface of the moon for only a few minutes. We had picked up the contingency rock sample and were preparing to begin our other duties. But a man at Houston Control, watching us on his television screen, saw something wrong with my spacesuit.

Houston: "Dave, this is Houston. Be advised Jim's got a flap hanging from the lower right-hand corner of his backpack which perhaps you could button up the next time you are close to him."

Scott: "Okay. It's his water flap."

Irwin: "Yes, I can see that in the shadow."

The interesting parallel in the Christian's life is: Just as Houston was able to see something that needed adjustment on my spacesuit, so is the ever-present Holy Spirit, our Companion and Comforter, always able to help us with our spiritual problems.

When Jesus left the earth physically, he promised not to leave the disciples alone without help. He knew his absence would leave a devastating and shattering void. The disciples would miss him and his continuing counsel. So he said, "And I will ask the Father, and he will give you another Counselor to be with you forever—the Spirit of truth. The world cannot accept him, because it neither sees him nor knows him. But you will know him, for he lives with you and will be in you. I will not leave you as orphans" (John 14:16-18).

As always-present Houston helped us at all times, so does the Holy Spirit. Jesus says, "But the Counselor, the Holy Spirit, whom the Father will send in my name, will teach you all things and will remind you of everything I have said to you. But when he, the Spirit of truth, comes, he will guide you into all truth" (John 14:26; 16:13).

This extra dimension of the Holy Spirit in our lives is "God in us," which is the dynamic and vitality of our Christian experience. "For God did not give us a spirit of timidity, but a spirit of power, of love and of self-discipline" (2 Tim. 1:7).

15
Are You Scented with the Fragrance of Christ?

When we climbed back into the Lunar Module after our first day of walking on the moon, we were overwhelmed by a strong, acrid smell like gunpowder. We discovered that it was the lunar dust which covered us. Inside the spacecraft the dust had turned black from its exposure to oxygen for the first time, and the oxidation made it smell like gunpowder. The dust completely covered us, some of it so small that it penetrated even the tiniest pores on the spacesuit. You can look at my spacesuit today and see that it is still gray with lunar dust. Even with vacuuming, it wouldn't come out.

Second Corinthians 2:14-16 says, "But thanks be to God, who always leads us in triumphal procession in Christ and through us spreads everywhere the fragrance of the knowledge of him. For we are to God the aroma of Christ among those who are being saved and those who are perishing. To the one we are the smell of death; to the other, the fragrance of life."

Here are a comparison and a contrast. People exposed for the first time to Christians who are truly scented with the aroma of Christ are much like the lunar dust which is exposed to oxygen for the first time. Yet the fragrance of Christ is sweet, not acrid. All Christians should have a fragrance which penetrates and permeates every pore of the person we contact. The fragrance of life is one of love, gentleness, and holiness.

We Christians should be like Peter and John in Acts 4:13 of whom it was said, when observed by the leaders in Jerusalem, "And they took knowledge of them, that they had been with Jesus" (KJV).

MORE THAN EARTHLINGS   **41**

16
Each Day Is Brand New with Christ

The morning after our first night of sleep on the moon we could no longer smell the "gunpowder" odor of the lunar dust. During the night our atmosphere-scrubbing system gave us a brand-new, fresh environment. The lithium hydroxide cannisters which filtered all the oxygen had removed all the impurities. When we awakened it was with a new day of fresh oxygen—we started all over again.

Lamentations 3:22-23 observes, "Because of the Lord's great love we are not consumed, for his compassions never fail. They are new every morning; great is your faithfulness."

As with the oxidized lunar dust smell which passed in the night, so do our yesterdays with their evil, sin, and dirtiness. God is so infinitely compassionate that he does not consume us for what we do against him.

Each day with Christ will be a different one, a new one, a fresh one. Begin each day as a rededication to the Lord. How your day goes is often determined by how you start it. Reflect on God's compassions. Read a portion of the Scriptures each morning. Pray to God. Don't take this new day for granted.

Suppose you are on the moon. You wake up each morning and hear the gentle humming of the fans and pumps in the Lunar Module. You see the oxygen tanks that are giving you life. You use the communications system and computer control panel which connects you with the Command Module and with NASA back on earth. Not for one moment do you take all that for granted, for you are absolutely dependent upon those systems. And we are totally dependent on Him.

17
Should Man
Travel in Space?

I looked down and saw my footprints in the dust of the moon. They will be there forever, undisturbed, just as I left them. My footprints will be eternal testimony to Psalm 8:6, "You made him ruler over the works of your hands; you put everything under his feet." God made man the ruler of all His works.

God created man in His own image—a curious, dynamic, exploring man. We are truly that exploring creature. Dave Scott commented, as we were viewing the mountains of the moon, "As I stand out here viewing the wonders of the unknown at Hadley, I sort of realize there's a fundamental truth to our nature. Man must explore."

Some ask if man were meant to travel in space. Should he visit the moon and Mars? Some feel that if God had intended for man to be in space, he would have put him there. Actually, God already has placed man in space—on this beautiful, blue planet. Earth is much like a spaceship. It is moving through space. It has its own atmosphere system. It has a heat source. It is one of the planets of our solar system. We are already space creatures! It is a matter of perspective.

God has put us in charge of all his works, not only his works on earth, but even beyond the earth.

But as we explore outwardly, we must not forget that great frontier which exists for each person—his own self. A person must also rule self. Titus 1:7 uses the phrase, "master of himself."

MORE THAN EARTHLINGS

Jim Irwin looked down and photographed his footprints on the moon's surface (NASA Photo).

The entirety of the great chapter on love, 1 Corinthians 13—if you were to analyze it in detail—would show a tremendous amount of self-control. "Love is patient, love is kind. It does not envy, it does not boast, it is not proud. It is not rude, it is not self-seeking, it is not easily angered, it keeps no record of wrongs" (1 Cor. 13:4-5). The thrust of these words is: One should also be the ruler of his own self, the crowning point in all of God's creation.

18
How Big Is Your God?

While on the dark side of the moon we made our observations into deep space, looking for black holes, pulsars, and other phenomena. It was total darkness, like being down in a deep mine. Because there was nothing to reflect the light, we could view a vast array of stars out the spacecraft window, far more than can be seen from earth. There was none of the twinkling caused by the earth's atmosphere, so the stars were brilliant and unwavering—like a black cloth dotted with billions of stationary pinpoints of light.

Scientists have estimated that there are 100 billion stars in our galaxy alone, and an estimated 100 billion galaxies, each with at least as many stars as ours! This would make 10,000,-000,000,000,000,000,000 stars. To put this number into human perspective, it has been figured that if each person on earth were able to count 50 billion stars, there would still be billions uncounted!

Psalm 147:4 testifies of God, "He determines the number of the stars and calls them *each by name*" (italics mine). There are about 600,000 words in the English language, and only a small percentage of these are proper names. In fact, a book printed with names for babies, listed as "the most complete book of its kind," has only 6,500 names. Yet God has a name for each of the 100 billion billion stars!

God not only has names for all the stars, he also sees each sparrow fall (Matt. 10:29). He knows how many hairs are on the heads of each of almost five billion earthlings (Luke 12:7).

He is a detail-conscious God, but they aren't meaningless details to him. If he has thoughts for the countless stars, birds, and strands of hair, imagine how much he thinks about you as a person, for whom he sent his Son to die! Psalm 139:17-18 exclaims, "How precious also are thy thoughts unto me, O God! how great is the sum of them! If I should count them, they are more in number than the sand" (KJV).

How big is your view of God? First Kings 8:27 says, "But will God indeed dwell on the earth? behold, the heaven and heaven of heavens cannot contain thee; how much less this house that I have builded?" (KJV). Yes, we have an infinite God who cares about the finite you.

19
It Isn't Easy to Walk on the Moon

And I mean that literally. We fell down several times, tripping on unseen rocks hidden in the thick lunar dust. The footing was very unsure.

As the Christian travels through his life on earth, the footing here can also be tricky. This is why God is referred to as a Rock so often in the Old Testament. Psalm 18:2 asserts, "My God is my rock." Psalm 19:15 affirms, "The Lord is upright; he is my Rock."

Jesus' disciples had walked the rocky hillsides of Israel. They knew what it was to slip and fall on the unsure footing of the loose rocks strewn on the hills. Any Christian who has turned from the Lord, his Rock, knows how precarious life is when he is out of fellowship with God.

David had many difficult times. He fell into the slimy pit of sin when he stole another man's wife, then had that man killed. David sang in Psalm 40:1-3:

> I waited patiently for the Lord; he turned to me and heard my cry. He lifted me out of the slimy pit, out of the mud and mire; he set my feet on a rock and gave me a firm place to stand. He put a new song in my mouth, a hymn of praise to our God. Many will see and fear and put their trust in the Lord.

If you do slip and fall, hasten to return to the Lord. He will hear your cry of help. He promises to lift you out of the difficulty and will give you firm footing. You will be happy again. Others will see your change of life and will be able to trust in God because of it.

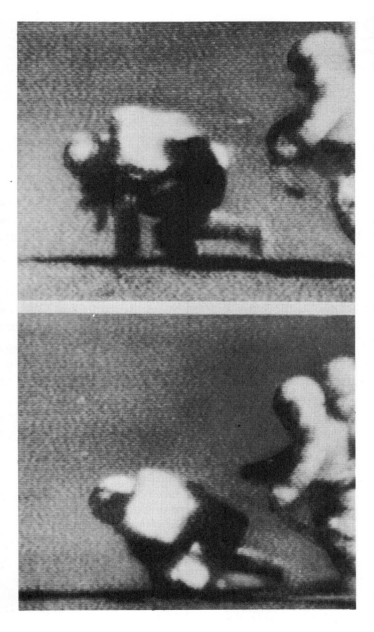

Astronaut Irwin rushed to assist Astronaut Scott who had fallen during a moonwalk *(NASA Photo).*

20
Creation

Most of the rocks previously brought back from the moon were dark, dense basalt. Scientists knew that if the moon were composed entirely of this dense rock, it could not possibly be in its present orbit. It would be too heavy. They knew there had to be an abundance of lighter material, lighter in density and color. Our mission was to find a lighter rock from the mountains on the moon.

While we were exploring, Dave said, "Jim, do you see what I see? I think we've found what we came for." We had located a pure, white rock, the oldest rock brought back from the moon—part of the deep internal material which had been ejected to make the mountains—and the most important scientific discovery of our mission.

The press labeled it the "Genesis" rock, for it confirmed the fact that the earth and moon were created at the same time, giving scientific proof of the creation story of Genesis 1:14-18:

> And God said, "Let there be lights in the expanse of the sky to separate the day from the night, and let them serve as signs to mark seasons and days and years, and let them be lights in the expanse of the sky to give light on the earth." And it was so. God made two great lights— the greater light to govern the day and the lesser light to govern the night. He also made the stars. God set them in the expanse of the sky to give light on the earth, to govern the day and the night, and to separate light from darkness. And God saw that it was good.

21
The Stability of a Violent Sun

One can't stare at the sun from earth, let alone from outer space where it is even more blinding. With no atmosphere to reduce the intensity, we saw the sun in all its power and glory.

When we needed to reduce the brightness of the sun inside the Lunar Module, we put an aluminized mylar cover over the windows. This helped create an artificial night so we could sleep. When out on the moon we had a gold-plated visor over our regular clear visor to screen out the pure energy, especially to keep the ultraviolet rays from hurting our eyes.

The sun is violent. Astronomers tell us that a shock wave from one storm center on the sun's surface can move a million miles in a few minutes and set off another storm. Explosions on the sun shoot nuclear eruptions millions of miles into space. Sun spots affect our weather, 93,000,000 miles away!

Yet, it is an amazingly stable star on a larger level. It is our source of life. We are exactly the right distance from it to provide sufficient heat to sustain life. The other planets are either too hot or too cold. In this sense, it is as the Lord is—a source of life and a giver of good gifts. Psalm 84:11 testifies, "For the Lord God is a sun and shield; he bestows favor and honor. No good thing does the Lord withhold from those who walk uprightly" (RSV).

Jesus is described as a healing sun of righteousness in Malachi 4:2. As the sun is health to us physically, the Son is health to us spiritually. Jesus declared, "I have come that they may have life, and have it to the full" (John 10:10).

He gives other gifts of spiritual health:

Joy—"I have told you this so that my joy may be in you and that your joy may be complete" (John 15:11).

Peace—"Peace I leave with you; my peace I give you. I do not give to you as the world gives. Do not let your hearts be troubled and do not be afraid" (John 14:27).

Eternal life—"He who has the Son has life; he who does not have the Son of God does not have life" (1 John 5:12).

Love—"For I am convinced that neither death nor life, neither angels nor demons, neither the present nor the future, nor any powers, neither height nor depth, nor anything else in all creation, will be able to separate us from the love of God that is in Christ Jesus our Lord" (Rom. 8:38-39).

If you have Christ within you, you have all this.

22
There Are No
Secrets in Space

Everything Astronauts say in space is heard. Everything!

Even when we were on the backside of the moon, where there is a one-hour communications blockage, everything Dave, Al, and I said was heard. It was picked up on an on-board recorder, which Houston controlled. They could play it back anytime they wanted. There are no secrets in space!

The Father knows all. God knows everything that is happening in the recesses of our hearts—in the distances of space, even on the backside of the moon. Psalm 139:1-6 says,

> *O Lord, you have searched me and you know me. You know when I sit and when I rise; you perceive my thoughts from afar. You discern my going out and my lying down; you are familiar with all my ways.* Before a word is on my tongue you know it completely, O Lord. *You hem me in, behind and before; you have laid your hand upon me. Such knowledge is too wonderful for me, too lofty for me to attain.*

We stand amazed at the technology it takes to launch man in space, but think of the magnificent God we adore and worship. Long before radios and tape recorders and man's technology, there were no secrets between God and man. And this God who knows all our words before we even speak them is the same God who loves us so much he sent his Son to die for us, so we could be *with him* for all eternity. This mighty God is worthy of our adoration. We should bow before him and give him all the glory.

23
God Does Answer Prayer

Our moon exploration used the first surface transportation ever designed for another planet. It was the lunar dunes buggy named Rover. It was supposed to have front- and rear-wheel steering, but during our first day on the moon we had only rear-wheel steering. Neither we nor Houston could locate the problem.

The second day we came out and miraculously the front-wheel steering worked. Switches were exactly as they had been left the night before. Dave marveled at it, too. In fact, he jokingly commented that people must have come up during the night and fixed it. We were amazed that it had changed overnight. But it was an answer to prayer. James 5:16 says, "The prayer of a righteous man is powerful and effective."

God does supernaturally become involved in the small details of our lives. We had another problem that first day during our lunar exploration. We had to assemble the Central Station of the Apollo Lunar Surface Experiments Package (ALSEP). The Central Station was the nerve center which relayed data back to earth for all the scientific experiments we left up there. I had to erect this station.

If all the bolts were released correctly the station would spring up when the last bolt and two cotter pins were removed. I loosened the last bolt; then, using a small hand tool, pulled the string attached to the cotter pins. The string broke! So there we were—the Central Station was sitting on the surface of the moon, and I couldn't get two little cotter pins out with my bulky gloves.

What would I do? The Central Station was the key to all the scientific experiments. The problem was time, an extremely limited commodity while exploring on the moon. We were already behind schedule. I prayed to God, "Show me the right way the first time." We were taught not to use our fingers when working with the sensitive equipment; not only were the spacesuit gloves bulky, but the scientists were fearful we might damage the equipment. We had specialized tools for each job.

I felt the Lord wanted me to get down on my knees and work the cotter pins loose with my fingers, bulky gloves and all. I tried it, the pins released, and the Central Station popped right up.

Matthew 21:22 promises, "If you believe, you will receive whatever you ask for in prayer."

24
Special Nourishment for the Christian

After the first few hours out on the surface of the moon, I was tired, exhausted, hungry, and thirsty. I never would have made it through that day without a little nourishment. We had food sticks about twelve inches long that extended up into our helmets. The stick was positioned so we could reach down, grab it with our mouths, and take a bite. I had gobbled mine down after the traverse, and it had given me energy to put up the science station.

We face the same situation each day as Christians. We need sustenance for our spiritual lives. Spiritual food, however, is the Word of God.

Jesus is the living Word. John 1:1 and 1:14 record, "In the beginning was the Word, and the Word was with God, and the Word was God. . . . The Word became flesh and lived for a while among us. We have seen his glory, the glory of the one and only Son, who came from the Father, full of grace and truth." What can Jesus do through the Word?

He quenches our thirst and satisfies our hunger. He teaches us, "I am the bread of life. He who comes to me will never go hungry, and he who believes in me will never be thirsty. This is the bread that came down from heaven . . . he who feeds on this bread will live forever" (John 6:35,58).

How do we appropriate this special food and drink? The Bible is the written Word. Through the Scriptures we get this nourishment. The Bible helps us grow. First, there is milk: First Peter 2:2 says, "As newborn babes, desire the sincere milk of the word, that ye may grow thereby" (KJV). This milk is for less mature Christians. There is also meat for the more mature:

> In fact, though by this time you ought to be teachers, you need someone to teach you the elementary truths of God's word all over again. You need milk, not solid food! Anyone who lives on milk, being still an infant, is not acquainted with the teaching about righteousness. But solid food is for the mature, who by constant use have trained themselves to distinguish good from evil (Heb. 5:12-14).

Are you daily taking the Scriptures into your life by reading, studying, hearing, memorizing, and meditating? Jeremiah 15:16 says, "Thy words were found, and I ate them, and thy words became to me a joy and the delight of my heart" (RSV).

We constantly referred to the checklists on our spacesuit sleeves *(NASA Photo).*

25
Wear a Spiritual Checklist on Your Cuff

When we left the Lunar Module and walked out on the surface of the moon, we had so many things to do that we fastened a "checklist" to our cuffs. The check list was a complete plan for surface operation bound into a pad and attached to the spacesuit sleeve. It told us what to do minute by minute. As we finished one page, we turned to the next. It gave us the proper order for unfastening bolts, removing dust covers, using our tools, and all sorts of other specific details. It was invaluable, since it was a guideline for the day's activities.

The journey through life is much like the moon walk in this sense, for we need a guide to assist us through the problems, the questions, and many of the decisions of each day. We need some sort of "cuff checklist," and we have it in the Word of God.

Second Timothy 3:16-17 emphasizes that, "All scripture is inspired by God and profitable for teaching, for reproof, for correction, and for training in righteousness, that the man of God may be complete, equipped for every good work." The Scriptures are a "complete" checklist for the Christian.

There are five ways to take the Word into one's life: meditation, memory, reading, studying, and hearing. Memory is the closest to the spacesuit cuff checklist, for then we always have it wherever we are and are prepared for any event. Psalm 119:9,11 says, "Wherewithal shall a young man cleanse his way? by taking heed thereto according to thy word. Thy word have I hid in mine heart, that I might not sin against thee."

26
Christ Is the
Master Source

In space one can't survive without being attached—in one way or another—to something else. This was true in several ways. When we left the Command Module and went down to the moon in the Lunar Module, we had no way to get back to earth *except* to return to the Command Module, which kept circling the moon for the three days Dave Scott and I were on the moon's surface.

The Command Module was built like a space-going tank (the shielding on it had to be able to withstand temperatures of up to 5,000 degrees), but the Lunar Module was an extremely fragile craft, incapable of reentering the earth's atmosphere. It was more like an aluminum can. In fact, when it was pressurized, the walls crinkled just like squeezing a soft drink can.

It makes me think of John 15:5, "I am the vine, you are the branches. He who abides in me, and I in him, he it is that bears much fruit, for apart from me you can do nothing" (RSV).

One of the fruits or results of our mission was the rocks we brought back from the mountains of the moon, the first such rocks ever recovered (all other rocks were from the plains). But without the connection with the Command Module, we could not have returned with those rocks. We would have been deserted forever on the moon.

The Christian can do *nothing* unless he is connected to his true life-support system, which is Christ. Philippians 4:13 says, "I can do everything through him who gives me strength," but apart from him we can do nothing.

We checked in with Al Worden in the Command Module each night before going to sleep—to make sure he was still there. That Command Module was our only way back to earth. It was reassuring each evening to know that all was well with Al.

The way we maintain an abiding posture in Christ is to talk to him by prayer and for him to talk to us by his Word. This is the basic hook-up of the branch to the vine. Do it daily and you will bring forth fruit for him.

27
Don't Put Your Friends in "Blackout"

While in space we were farther away from home than earthlings have ever been. The journey was fraught with danger; hundreds of mishaps could happen at any time. We were extremely busy, consumed with technical matters: numbers, computer readings, scientific assignments, photography, gauges, check lists.

Yet, in the midst of this billion-dollar technological adventure, Houston Control read me a telegram from my dad, mom, and brother. They reminisced about a trip we had taken together to the top of Mt. Whitney. They said they were proud of me and were with me in spirit. This touch from home—this good news from a far place—was a great morale booster. Proverbs 25:25 says, "As cold waters to a thirsty soul, so is good news from a far country."

Also, my family continually received "good news" about the flight—safe lift-off, proper engine correction burns, safe moon landing, safe lift-off from the moon, safe hookup with the command module—it was all as cold water to their thirsty, parched lips.

If the entire flight had been blacked out and only the few in Houston Control had known of our status, not only would my family and friends have been concerned, but also the millions of Americans (who paid for the trip) would have been anxious about the progress of the journey.

This makes me realize the priceless ministry of keeping in touch with family and friends who are far away. Take seriously Jesus' words in Matthew 10:42!

28
The Reality of the Invisible

Cosmic particles, which do not reach the earth because of the protection of our atmosphere and the Van Allen radiation belt, constantly bombarded us in outer space. The particles would penetrate the spacecraft, our spacesuits, and go right on through our bodies. But the only time we "saw" them was when they actually passed through the retina at the back of our eyes.

One time Dave, Al, and I were sitting side by side, and an extremely high energy particle came through the left side of the Command Module and passed through all of us. We each recorded it as it created a brilliant streak across the retina and went out the other side of the ship.

When we would lie down to sleep at night, instead of counting sheep, we would count flashes or streaks. It was a streak when it came from the side, a flash when it came directly at us. We were constantly in a vast ocean of particles, but only "saw" the ones which hit the retina. Though we couldn't see the billions of others, they were real, nonetheless.

As Christians we often fall into the trap of believing that the only "real" things are the ones we can "see," like fame, riches, power, leadership, applause, and awards. All of these are attractive. We long for them. Or we want to have the ministry another has. Or we want another's gift. Second Corinthians 4:18 shows us a better way, "So we fix our eyes not on what is seen, but on what is unseen. For what is seen is temporary, but what is unseen is eternal."

We must beware that the things of real value don't go past us unseen, missing the retina of our spiritual eyes. Matthew 6:19-21 urges:

> Do not store up for yourselves treasures on earth, where moth and rust destroy, and where thieves break in and steal. But store up for yourselves treasures in heaven, where moth and rust do not destroy, and where thieves do not break in and steal. For where your treasure is, there your heart will be also.

The real treasures are like these: when we love someone, even though we are not loved in return; when we give and the giver is never revealed; when we forgive someone who has betrayed us; when we smile where another would frown; when we understand where another would criticize. The "unseen" things are eternal.

29
Start Right—Finish Well

Sometimes I'm a bit impetuous. When we boarded the lunar dunes buggy, the Rover, for the first time, my seat belt didn't fit. Dave started to help me fix it. I said, "Don't waste time on it. I'll just hang on."

Dave said, "No, let's start out right. We've got too far to go."

He was right. There is a certain way of doing something that will most likely result in success. It should be done in a way which would gain the goal or prize. First Corinthians 9:24 asks, "Do you not know that in a race all the runners run, but only one gets the prize? Run in such a way as to get the prize." There was a right way to ride the Rover—it was to be properly strapped in.

When the Rover hit rocks it literally flew through space because of the lighter gravity—so it was important to have the seat belts fastened.

And, I guarantee you, we are going to hit some rocks as we live this Christian life. One must be properly strapped in with the basics of Christian living (a Christ-centered attitude, prayer, the Word, witnessing, fellowship, and obedience). When we hit those rough moments, we will be prepared.

30
The Fragility of Man

As spacemen: Man is amazingly strong, yet unbelievably fragile. He is strong (and intelligent) enough to put a spacecraft on a hostile planet, yet he has to be protected from that hostility (+215° F lunar noontime heat and −250° lunar nighttime cold) by a spacesuit. If my suit had been torn, my blood would have boiled! We needed the armor of a spacesuit.

As men: I couldn't imagine that I, a "hotshot" test pilot and Astronaut who had walked on the moon, would have a heart attack. I thought that was for people who ate and drank too much, smoked, and didn't exercise. It was hard to accept it when I had a heart attack. I was honestly embarrassed. It made me more dependent upon the Lord and made me accept my own human weakness. I needed the armor of strengthened heart muscles by proper diet and exercise.

As Christians: Even though we have God, the Word, and the power of the Holy Spirit, we Christians also need a special kind of armor. Ephesians 6:10-11 says, "Finally, be strong in the Lord and in His mighty power. Put on the full armor of God so that you can take your stand against the devil's schemes."

This assemblage of armor is a buckle of truth, a breastplate of righteousness, shoes of readiness to spread the gospel of peace, a shield of faith, a helmet of salvation, and a sword of the Spirit (the Word of God).

Take a personal inventory and see where you stand. Are you fully fitted with this suit of armor?

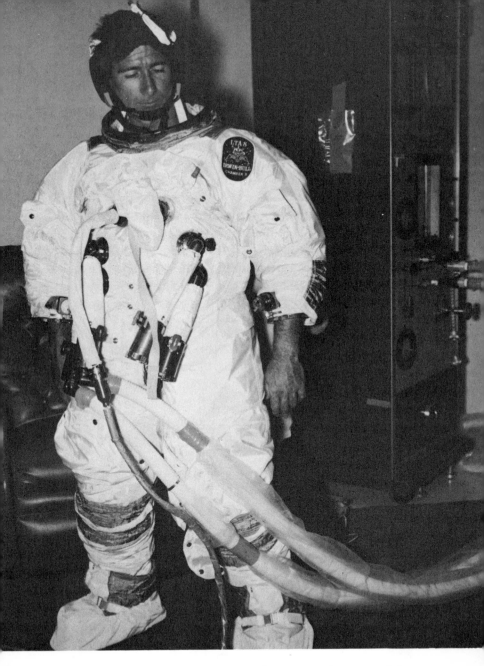

Irwin suited up for ingress-egress demonstration test with a Lunar Module (NASA Photo).

31
The Fearful Christian

We like to say, "Astronauts are never afraid." There are reasons we didn't live and work in constant fear, though we were in an extremely hazardous duty situation.

Fear, I believe, comes from incomplete knowledge. It comes because of uncertainty of the outcome. There are at least five reasons why we in the space program were able to handle fear, and parallels of these reasons can apply to the fearful Christian:

1. *We could deal with fear because we had thought through the results of anything that might happen.* Jesus tells us to do the same thing—to count the cost of being his disciple. In Luke 28-30 he says, "Suppose one of you wants to build a tower. Will he not first sit down and estimate the cost to see if he has enough money to complete it? For if he lays the foundation and is not able to finish it, everyone who sees it will ridicule him, saying, 'This fellow began to build and was not able to finish.'"

2. *We thought "success" to the point that we never imagined the possibility of defeat.* Paul teaches this in Philippians 4:13, "I can do everything through him who gives me strength."

3. *Being busy all the time helped us combat undue fear.* Colossians 3:23 advises, "Whatever you do, work at it with all your heart."

4. *We were totally dedicated.* We believed in the mission from the very depths of our beings. We felt it was the most

important task we could do with our lives and were willing to give even our lives if necessary. Paul wrote: "For to me, to live is Christ and to die is gain" (Phil. 1:21).

5. *We had faith in our resources, in all the research, in the people and equipment that helped launch us.* And, as Christians, we have faith in the resources of God. Philippians 4:19 says, "And my God will meet all your needs according to his glorious riches in Christ Jesus."

So, Christian, as Jesus counseled in Luke 12:32, "Do not be afraid, little flock, for your Father has been pleased to give you the kingdom."

32
Do All Things Heartily

Men do strange things to accomplish an objective. One of our missions was to drill a ten-foot-long core of rock from the moon. It was unbelievably strenuous. Dave operated the drill. Every one of his fingernails turned black because of the pressure he exerted. It was excruciating pain to push the drill down. Then, on the same operation, he pulled a muscle in his lower back.

We were determined to gather that rock core, for the many layers would be quite revealing to the scientists.

I knew we would get it out. Once I became involved in it, after seeing Dave's persistence, I was determined to stay there and dig it up, no matter the cost.

But how well do we as Christians work for the Lord? We should give it as much effort—in fact, more. Colossians 3:23-24 says, "Whatever you do, work at it with all your heart, as working for the Lord, not as men. . . . It is the Lord Christ you are serving."

Do we work hard for man, but give second best for the Lord? First Corinthians 15:58 reassures us, "Always give yourselves fully to the work of the Lord, because you know that your labor in the Lord is not in vain."

With Mount Hadley in the background, Irwin made a trench in the lunar soil *(NASA Photo).*

33
The Mountains
of the Moon

Apollo 15 was the first and only mission to explore the mountains of the moon. I had hoped that sometime during my time there I could quote an appropriate verse of scripture which would draw mens' thoughts to God.

On one of our drives in the lunar rover, Dave had a lyrical moment. He exulted, "Look at the mountains when they are all sunlit. Isn't that beautiful?"

I replied, "Dave, that reminds me of a favorite biblical passage in the Psalms: 'I will lift up mine eyes unto the hills, from whence cometh my help.' But, of course, we get quite a bit from Houston, too."

Walter Cronkite picked up on this and read all of Psalm 121 to the world-wide audience watching on television.

I didn't quote the next verse from that Psalm, which goes, "My help cometh from the Lord, which made heaven and earth." God made it possible for this entire mission to take place, and I realized that my help did come from him, who made heaven, the earth, and the moon.

He gave me then, and is giving me now, the spiritual help I need to sustain my flight for him, as his servant, to reach out to my fellow earthlings and tell them about the One who made heaven and earth.

34
Man Is Less
Than a Speck

When I stood on the moon and held my hand up to frame the earth between my thumb and forefinger, as one does to size something, the earth was the size of a marble. Man, on that gorgeous blue marble, was much less than a speck.

William Beebe, the marvelous naturalist, told the story of how he and Theodore Roosevelt had a little astronomical ritual they would often perform after an evening of deep conversation. They would go out on the lawn and search the skies. "We searched," Beebe says, "until we found, with or without glasses, the faint heavenly spot of light-mist beyond the lower left-hand corner of the Great Square of Pegasus, when one or the other of us would then recite:

'That is the Spiral Galaxy in Andromeda.
It is as large as our Milky Way.
It is one of a hundred million galaxies.
It is 750,000 light years away.
It consists of a hundred billion suns,
      each larger than our sun.'

"After an interval Colonel Roosevelt would grin at me and say: 'Now I think we are small enough! Let's go to bed.'"

The Psalmist asked, "When I consider your heavens, the work of your fingers, the moon and the stars, which you have set in place, what is man that you are mindful of him, the son of man that you care for him?" (Ps. 8:3-4).

That mindfulness of us is unfathomable. Paul writes of Christ, in Philippians 2:6-8:

Who, being in very nature God, did not consider equality with God something to be grasped, but made himself nothing, taking the very nature of a servant, being made in human likeness. And being found in appearance as a man, he humbled himself and became obedient to death—even death on a cross!

And that death on the cross was for us—to give us eternal life and forgiveness of our sins. Even though we are small, God has given us the capacity, the desire, and the way to know him. The Way was through Christ's death. He stated, "I am the way." (John 14:6). So man, less than a speck, becomes strategic in the universe—so important that Christ died for him.

35
Forgiving and Asking for Forgiveness

One of the tasks we carried out on the moon was what we called "The Galileo Experiment." Dave Scott dropped a falcon's feather from one hand and his rock hammer from the other. The point was to prove Galileo's argument that any two dropped objects will land at the same time in a vacuum, which had never been demonstrated. What would be more appropriate than to try it on the moon?

Dave performed the experiment. The hammer and feather floated down side by side, hitting the ground precisely at the same time, 1.3 seconds later.

I played a role in the experiment, too. After it was concluded and the TV cameras were turned off, I went about my business I was to do that day. In the process I accidently stepped on the feather, crushing it into the deep lunar dust. We never did find it. Dave had taken the feather from the falcon mascot at the Air Force Academy and wanted to keep it as a souvenir. He really became perturbed with me.

We all made a number of mistakes on the flight. I made them before the launch, during the flight, on the moon, and when we returned. Because of my spiritual reawakening during the flight, I knew I needed to ask forgiveness of Dave Scott, the commander of Apollo 15. Jesus instructed, "Therefore, if you are offering your gift at the altar and there remember that your brother has something against you, leave your gift there in front of the altar. First go and be reconciled to your brother; then come and offer your gift."

After Dave and I both retired from the military, we rarely saw each other in the United States, but our paths crossed in England from time to time. On one of those occasions, I asked his forgiveness for the mistakes I had made. He forgave me. I wonder who I will have to ask forgiveness of next?

Asking forgiveness of others and forgiving others aren't "extras" to do if you feel like it; they are part and parcel of being a Christian. It is part of everyday, normal Christian living. Colossians 3:13 says, "Bear with each other and forgive whatever grievances you may have against one another. Forgive as the Lord forgave you."

36
A Plaque for Some Unique Heroes

In a small crater about twenty feet away from where the Rover will be forever parked on the moon is a memorial to fourteen deceased American and Soviet spacemen. The memorial consists of a plaque which has all their names in alphabetical order and a small figure representing a fallen astronaut. Dave Scott observed, when placing the memorial, "Many people have contributed to this pinnacle we've reached, and we know of fourteen individuals who contributed all they had." These fourteen are commended and memorialized for their contribution to the space program.

Christians as well have a commendation list. It is in the eleventh chapter of Hebrews. "These were all commended for their faith" (Heb. 11:39).

This is the chapter which is the roll call of those men and women throughout biblical history who *believed in the promises of God*. They are called the "heroes of faith."

Why is faith so important? Hebrews 11:6 says, "And without faith it is impossible to please God, because anyone who comes to him must believe that *he exists* and that *he rewards* those who earnestly seek him" (italics mine).

You want to please God? Then believe in him.

In fact, if you earnestly seek him, he will *reward* you. One of these rewards is the abundant life Jesus promises in John 10:10, and the Scriptures are filled with rewards for the faithful.

And what is this faith based on? It "is being sure of what we hope for and certain of what we do not see. By faith we

**The Apollo 15 crew left this plaque memorializing all astro-
nauts and cosmonauts who have died during their space
programs (NASA Photo).**

understand that the universe was formed at God's command, so that what is seen was not made out of what was visible" (Heb. 11:1,3).

The entire Christian experience is based on faith—it is even called the Christian "faith." How is your faith? Do you believe in what you do not see, or are you waiting for proof, for a sign? You can please God by believing in him—by faith.

37
The Nonconformity of the Christian

There I was—on the moon—the end product of a multi-million-dollar space launch, and I was scooping dirt back between my legs like a dog does when digging under a fence. It was an undignified way for an Astronaut to act, but because of the awkwardness of the spacesuit, the lighter gravity of the moon, and the equipment I was using, I had no choice but to dig in this nonconforming manner. I was digging a trench about twelve inches deep to measure the cohesiveness of the soil, among other experiments.

However, as Christians, our whole lives are lived on a nonconformist level, for we live by faith, not by sight. Romans 12:2 admonishes, "Do not conform any longer to the pattern of this world, but be transformed by the renewing of your mind. Then you will be able to test and approve what God's will is—his good, pleasing and perfect will."

The world's pattern is to trust the balance in the bank account; the Christian's pattern is to trust God. Jesus said:

> So do not worry, saying, "What shall we eat?" or "What shall we drink?" or "What shall we wear?" For the pagans run after all these things, and your heavenly Father knows that you need them. But seek first his kingdom and his righteousness, and all these things will be given to you as well (Matt. 6:31-33).

Another example of the world's pattern is to be suspect of prayer, for it is talking to something "invisible." It is difficult for people to pray to a God they can't see. But Christians are of a different kingdom. Paul declared, in 2 Corinthians 10:2, that we do not live by "the standards of this world." For Christians believe James, when he wrote, "The prayer of a righteous man is powerful and effective" (James 5:16).

How then does one "renew" his mind? It is by allowing Christ and the richness of his Word to fill one's mind. Colossians 3:16 says, "Let the word of Christ dwell in you richly. . . ." What does this Word do within one's mind? Hebrews 4:12 says, "The word of God is living and active. Sharper than any double-edged sword, it penetrates even to dividing soul and spirit, joints and marrow; it judges the thoughts and attitudes of the heart."

38
Beware of the
"Fireball Effect"

We mentioned on page 53 that communications with Houston Control were impossible when we went around the backside of the moon.

But there was also another time when there was a total loss of communications with Mission Control. It lasted for four minutes when we reentered the earth's atmosphere. When we hit the resistance of the atmosphere about fifty miles from earth, the spaceship nose cone heated up to 5,000° F., creating a "fireball effect." This ionized sheath of particles prevented all communications.

As Christians, we sometimes move through life so fast, even when doing ministry, that we hit this wall of noncommunication with God. Because of our very busyness, we don't pray and don't take time to meditate on God's Word. We lose touch with him. We are moving too fast. The psalmist says, in Psalm 46:10, "Be still, and know that I am God."

This is why it is so imperative to maintain a daily time of quiet—when we can push aside all the haste and noise of living and sit down with Him to quietly pray and read the Scriptures. It doesn't have to be lengthy; but communications do need to be established. Even if brief, your quiet time should be unhurried.

Maybe you are at the "fireball effect." Then Jesus says,

Come to me, all you who are weary and burdened, and I will give you rest. Take my yoke upon you and learn from me, for I am gentle and humble in heart, and you will find rest for your souls. For my yoke is easy and my burden is light (Matt. 11:28-30).

39
Does God Exist?

When the first Russian Cosmonaut, Yuri Gagarin, returned to earth, he traveled widely and told everyone, "I did not see God up there." The second Russian in space, Titov, also boasted that he was an eagle and could not see God anywhere.

I heard about a twelve-year-old girl in Gothenburg, Sweden, who was so troubled by Gagarin's statement that she wrote him a letter. It was simple and to the point:

> Dear Cosmonaut Gagarin: I understand that you have flown in space and that you say you did not see God. Sir, I just want to ask you if you are pure in your heart?

These words from a young girl express wisdom beyond her years. She was sharing the words of Christ when he said in Matthew 5:8, "Blessed are the pure in heart, for they will see God."

I believe we see what our hearts let us see. When we have a pure heart we can then receive what God has in store for us—his rich blessings. We can see God in all of life. We can receive his pure light. I sensed the presence of God in space. I wanted to return to earth to share God's love with earthlings.

When I visited Egypt in January of 1975, I learned that I was the first American Astronaut to visit there. Gagarin had been there much earlier. The members of the Egyptian press were eager to have him say something about the spiritual impact of his space venture. Gagarin rebuffed them with, "I did not see God there." Now my mission to that country and to all countries which I visit is to share the love of God.

When on the moon I was so inspired by the presence of the Lord that I quoted Psalm 121:1, "I will lift up mine eyes unto the hills from whence cometh my help" (KJV). And on Christmas eve of 1968 when Apollo 8 circled the moon and was on the backside of the moon, we heard them read the Genesis account of creation, "In the beginning God created the heaven and the earth." The listening earth sat spellbound as we were reminded of God's goodness to the men of the blue planet.

Does God exist? The pure in heart will see God.

40
Develop a Sane Estimate of Yourself

Because of the moon flight I have had the opportunity to meet people like Golda Meier and Anwar Sadat—and the heads of state of Belgium, Vietnam, Jordan, Great Britain, South Africa, the Irish Republic, and the United States. Proverbs 22:29 says, "Do you see a man skilled in his work? He will serve before kings."

This can easily turn one's head. We are not to become too enamored with the royalty of this earth. Job 34:18-20 says, "Is he not the One who says to kings, 'You are worthless,' and to nobles, 'You are wicked,' who shows no partiality to princes and does not favor the rich over the poor, for they are all the work of his hands? They die in an instant, in the middle of the night . . . " We must remember that we are children of the King of kings and the Prince of peace, Jesus Christ.

You may have a skill which brings you before leaders, the rich, the great. If so, "Do not think of yourself more highly than you ought, but rather think of yourself with sober judgment . . . Do not be proud, but be willing to associate with people of low position. Do not be conceited" (Rom. 12:3,16).

I will be with God for eternity—but not because I was an Astronaut, not because I was one of twelve men to walk on the moon. Those feats have absolutely nothing to do with it. Ephesians 2:8-9 makes it plain: "For it is by grace you have been saved, through faith—and this not from yourselves, it is the gift of God—not by works, so that no one can boast."

41
A Workman
Approved by God

On the way back from the moon, Al Worden had to take a sixteen-minute "space walk" to retrieve two cassettes of film from the Scientific Instrument Module (SIM). The film contained views of the moon as Endeavour cruised in lunar orbit. These had to be brought in, or they would have been lost when the service module, in which the SIM bay was located, was discarded as the Endeavour neared Earth.

I was to film him doing this, but I goofed up. When I hooked my suit umbilicals, I wrapped them the wrong way around the strut. This gave me less freedom of movement and I couldn't get out of the hatch as far as I should have been able to. I took the pictures, but not from the vantage point I was supposed to be in.

I simply hadn't hooked up my equipment properly!

Christians, as Astronauts must, need to use their equipment properly. Since we are soldiers of Christ, one of our primary pieces of "equipment" is the Word of God. In Hebrews it is called a "two-edged sword." In Ephesians it is called the "sword of the Spirit."

Paul tells Timothy that this piece of equipment must be "correctly" handled: "Do your best to present yourself to God as one approved, a workman who does not need to be ashamed and who correctly handles the word of truth" (2 Tim. 2:15). Later in that same letter, Paul wrote, "All Scripture is God-breathed and is useful for teaching, rebuking, correcting and training in righteousness, so that the man of

God may be thoroughly equipped for every good work" (2 Timothy 3:16).

To handle a sword properly, one must practice with it (as an Astronaut practices hooking up his umbilicals!). Study it, read it, meditate on it, hear it, and memorize it. Do as the Bereans did: "Now the Bereans were of more noble character than the Thessalonians, for they received the message with great eagerness and *examined the Scriptures every day* to see if what Paul said was true" (Acts 17:11). Learn to use your sword adroitly. It is the Word of God. It can change others; it can change you. Be a workman approved by God.

42
Is There Life in Outer Space?

During our flight we saw numerous "unidentified flying objects" (UFO's). The question is: What were they? I think they are easily explained, though rumors persist that we saw strange objects in space. If you were to ask all of the Astronauts, I don't think any of them would say they saw something like an extra-terrestrial spacecraft.

In most cases the UFO's were probably parts of our own spacecraft which had peeled loose and were following us. Also, anytime we dumped fluids, they would immediately freeze and form ice crystals in a variety of shapes. When the sun reflected on them, we saw all the colors of the spectrum. With this huge cloud of crystals flying with us, we were always looking through a kind of kaleidoscope of magnificent color—we would look out into the blackness of space and see these rainbow-colored particles which seemed to stretch on forever.

Before man ever traveled into space, he asked, "Is there life out there?" Now that we have the capability of space exploration, it is asked even more frequently.

However, there is a more basic question: Do we really have *life*, the real life God wants us to have, right here on earth? Are we appropriating all of God's blessings here and now? This is far more significant than what we will find in outer space.

Second Corinthians 5:17 says, "Therefore, if anyone is in Christ, he is a new creation; the old has gone, the new has come!" Not only does God give us eternal life, but he transforms us into new creations—right here, right now—even while we remain earthlings on this planet!

43
The Return of
Jesus Christ

When we came back from the moon and were again caught in the earth's gravity, we were plummeting toward the South Pacific at thousands of miles per hour. The resistance of the atmosphere slowed us down, and finally at 10,000 feet our parachutes opened and we gently floated toward our splashdown target zone.

Military helicopters hovered nearby to monitor our descent. At 2,000 feet we went through a cloud bank and when we came through the clouds, we were right in the midst of a group of the helicopters. In fact, one pilot looked up and there we were, almost on top of him! What an awesome and surprising moment that must have been for him: looking up and seeing a spacecraft descending right above him!

This will always be a strong lesson to me regarding the return of Christ. He will descend just as he ascended. Acts 1:9-11 says:

> After he said this, he was taken up before their very eyes, and a cloud hid him from their sight. They were looking intently up into the sky as he was going, when suddenly two men dressed in white stood beside them. "Men of Galilee," they said, "why do you stand here looking into the sky? This same Jesus, who has been taken from you into heaven, will come back in the same way you have seen him go into heaven."

Jesus himself describes his return:

> For as the lightning comes from the east and flashes to

MORE THAN EARTHLINGS 89

the west, so will be the coming of the Son of Man. They will see the Son of Man coming on the clouds of the sky, with power and great glory. No one knows about that day or hour, not even the angels in heaven, nor the Son, but only the Father. Therefore, keep watch, because you do not know on what day your Lord will come. So you also must be ready, because the Son of Man will come at an hour when you do not expect him (Matt. 24:24,30,36,42,44).

I think of that helicopter pilot who looked up in utter amazement to see the spaceship come down through the clouds so close to him. I must be ready and must live with the continual consciousness of the imminent return of Jesus Christ!

44
The Splendor of the Stars

The dazzling brilliance of the stars we saw from the backside of the moon makes me think of the Bible verses which say some strange and curious things about stars. These statements were made in advance of the recent scientific discoveries which give us up-to-date information about the stars.

First Corinthians 15:41 says, "The sun has one kind of splendor, the moon another and the stars another; and star differs from star in splendor." How could Paul know this? There were no telescopes. He looked up by the naked eye and saw the same stars you and I see.

We now know that stars aren't the same. They are classified by the letters O, B, A, F, G, K, M, R, N, and S. O is the hottest; S is the coolest. The sun is near the middle, a G star. These letters also indicate the color of the stars, the color determining the heat. For example, O, B, and A are bluish-white (or extremely hot); F and G are yellow; K is orange; and M, R, N, and S are different shades of red (the coolest).

And we've heard about the various sizes and shapes of stars: the dwarfs, twin stars, giants, pulsars, black holes, super-novas.

But there is something else coming to us from the stars, other than light—we are "hearing" things from space. Astronomers report that the radio telescopes are picking up a strange "whisper" from empty space, a weak, but continual microwave radiation coming from the sky, day and night. Psalm 19:1-2,4 says:

> *The heavens declare the glory of God; the skies proclaim the work of his hands. Day after day they pour forth speech; night after night they display knowledge. Their voice goes out into all the earth, their words to the ends of the world.*

How would the Psalmist know this? Hebrews 1:1 says, "In the past God spoke to our forefathers through the prophets at many times and in various ways." The inspired Word of God told earthlings things about space that we haven't scientifically "discovered" until recently. This is why we can trust the Word as a guide for our lives.

MORE THAN EARTHLINGS

45
The Most Important Thing on Earth— or in Space

The trip to the moon dramatically changed my life, as it did the lives of all the Astronauts who took that voyage. One can't help being changed by the fame, the glory, and the history of the event.

But there are far more important facts to consider in life than even a trip to the moon, however majestic and historic that is. In fact, I can quote with Paul, "But whatever was to my profit I now consider loss for the sake of Christ. What is more, I consider everything a loss compared to the surpassing greatness of knowing Christ Jesus my Lord." (Phil. 3:7-8a).

A personal relationship with Jesus Christ is the true beginning of the Christian life. All other events in one's existence pale in significance—even walking on the moon—compared to developing a daily, intimate relationship with Christ.

Can you imagine anything more dramatic or exciting than the God of creation entering into your very being? He does that through his Son, Jesus Christ, when you invite Christ into your life.

I believe Jesus Christ walking on the earth is far more important than man walking on the moon. Just as surely as he walked 2,000 years ago, he wants to walk today in your life. All you have to do is call upon him. He wants you to have life and have it more abundantly (John 10:10). You do this by acknowledging your need of a Savior. Your first prayer must be, "Lord, help me, a sinner," and then invite him into your life by faith. Jesus said, "I am the way, the truth, and the life. No man cometh unto the Father but by me" (John 14:6).

46
My Continuing
"High Flight"

My outer-space trip is over. Completed. I am now called a "former" astronaut; however, I am still on a High Flight. This is not a technically oriented journey—but a spiritual one. I bring the message of Jesus Christ to earthlings all around the world. "High Flight" is the name of the organization I head which sponsors this international ministry.

The name "High Flight" comes from the title of the well-known poem by John Gillespie Magee, Jr. The word "High" implying an elevation of spirit and motive, and "Flight" connoting activity and involvement in life.

The High Flight insignia (shown here) symbolically represents the mission of the ministry of High Flight, my non-profit Christian organization.

It shows two intersecting orbits around the earth. Each orbit has a high point, emphasizing the importance of elevated goals in man's outreach.

The *vertical* orbit represents the mutual search between God and man; the horizontal orbit represents man's outreach to other men; and the cross represents the Christ-centered principles embraced by the members of High Flight. This cross is placed at the intersection of the two orbits, signifying the crucial nature of Christ in resolving man's two greatest enigmas—his relationship with God and his relationship with his brother. (The insignia was designed by Astronaut Col. William Pogue.)

This book represents part of my message to earthlings. As

you read it and share it with others, remember that you, too, can be "more than earthlings." You can become a child of God by asking forgiveness of your sins and accepting Christ into your life as your personal Savior for those sins which separate you from God. John 1:12 says, "Yet to all who received him, to those who believed in his name, he gave the right to become the children of God." I invite you to make this decision.

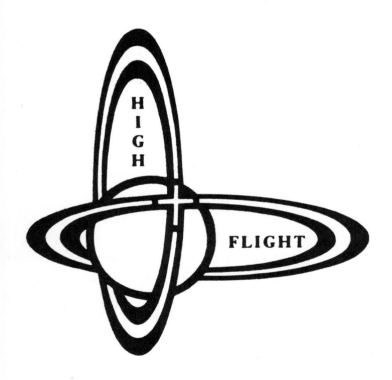